CALL SIGN STINGRAY

MEMOIR

non-fiction autobiography

First printing
Call Sign Stingray Memoir of the Crazy Colonel
17 September 2020
ISBN 978-1-7358144-0-7
Under the 45th President of the United States of America.

Second printing
Call Sign Stingray Memoir
15 October 2020
electronic version
ISBN 978-1-7358144-1-4
Print version
ISBN 978-1-7358144-2-1

"Let prejudices and local interest yield to reason"
"Let us look to our national character and to things beyond the present period. "
George Washington

Inscribed on the George Washington Masonic National Memorial.

PROLOGUE

Every community has it rules some written some unwritten some are never shared only learned. This is a story of how one person survived rapes, abuse, the general absurdity and cruelty of mankind. Portions of the story can only be verified by people who were there. It is a story about people backing people, both good and bad. Good and bad are sometimes the same people. A story about opportunities missed and taken.

Portions of this story are of horrific and traumatic events. Things which under no circumstances should be done to any being. The subject is of a mature nature and discretion shall be exercised.

Getting hit so hard a closed head wound is caused takes on an interesting medical progression. The first 30 minutes, first three hours, first three days, first three weeks. Everything past that is healing so long as the environment is conducive for healing to take place. Healing takes time and effort.

People seem to think sexual assault is sex. They leave out the assault portion. Some people seem to think it is a subject that should be mocked and abuse continued. That got me to the most messed up job I ever had, along the way I forgave one of my rapist. By not listening to a general I lost my marriage, ended on the wrong side of a literal Viper nest getting bit walking through it. Two guards took more of a hit, the big guy bit twice the skinny guy took three or four bites. We all stood there looking at that snake nursery with the nearest medical attention on the other side, feeling the pain of the bites sinking in. A decision was made to go the other way 500 yards to another place with medical help. That was a mistake with life changing consequences. If the reader thinks that is odd or messed up just wait; it gets better (or worse). I lost the guards in what was now a battlefield.

CONTINUUM OF FORCE

We fight as warriors and even in lives as civilians. We need to know when and how to increase and decrease the force we use. Ego and emotions have to be set aside regarding decisions of appropriate force. This is the hardest part, ego and emotions drive bad decisions.

When using force we begin with mere presence. Do we look like somebody that is easily overpowered or taken? Aware of our surroundings and responding appropriately? Do we present ourselves as hard or soft targets? Next on the continuum is verbal. Do we speak softly, sternly, quietly, loudly, peacefully or angrily? We spend every day of our lives using these first two levels of force; sometimes appropriately sometimes inappropriately. The majority of human beings never exceed this level of force in their entire life. It consists of how we present ourselves and how we speak. These first two steps are appropriate civil life. There is rarely a need to progress past this point.

The next steps move to physical aggression or defense; grasping pushing striking, taking physical control of another's body. Parents do it all the time keeping a toddler from running into the street. Unarmed self-defense or aggression is at this level. Further up the continuum are less lethal weapons, lethal weapons; knives guns tanks planes, nuclear weapons obliterating city's. All of which as human beings we have justified using.

Force is learned and trained. There's a difference between learning and training. I learned fighting bullies to get to school in my preteens, watching movies, watching Japanese police. I was trained at karate classes, the military, law-enforcement combative classes, from individuals who shared their learned and trained techniques.

In a fight there's a flow that comes naturally. This flow is independent per fight. It's either present or not. When this flow is not present the fight is an unorganized ineffective fumbling of force. When flow is present one movement flows into the next movement. The mind is full of thought, reassessing what needs to be done to remove whatever threat caused the fight. There's no hard kata to follow any technique from any discipline may be used. The thought process during a fight; is this working? If not change to something that works.

THROWING ROCKS

The south perimeter of NAS Miramar has Miramar Road on one side a chain-link fence with barbwire on top and a gravel single lane perimeter road. The perimeter Road was right behind housing. The field separating the road from housing was a great place for neighborhood kids to play. Granted the neighborhood was officers housing and the admiral preferred to not come home to all the neighborhood kids playing on his roof, even if it was the largest roof. In the heat of one of the days, a large group of kids including myself wandered bored around the perimeter road. Nothing to do but walk down this road until someone decided to throw a rock over the fence. Soon the entire group of kids were throwing rocks over the fence. They were landing on Miramar Road, hitting the occasional car. Sometimes a car would hit a rock and send it flying. After a while one of the older kids yelled "run"! I reached back to grab one last rock to throw over the fence. I grasped a hand sized rock but it wouldn't budge. I looked down at shiny black with a mirror shine, Attached to a blue leg with a red stripe running up the side, a white 45 caliber holster. I continue to look up past a tan arm, at the deep green cross rifles and three chevrons on his sleeve. Eyes locked onto mine, my eyes went wide. In a stern voice he said "DO NOT RUN". I froze but managed to glanced left to see all the other kids in the neighborhood, including the admirals son, running down the road 100 feet from me. The Marine grabbed me up by the scruff of my T-shirt and walked me to the gate house.

At the gate house a line of cars waited with flat tires. The Sergeant let me briefly meet this angry crowd of people. Then secured me in the gate house, asked who I was and who my dad was. I replied with the information and let him know my dad was a Lieutenant who outranked a mere Sergeant. The Sergeant called my dad at work and a few minutes later he showed up, got out of the family car then walked over to the Sergeant. In classic Marine fashion the Sergeant saluted my dad and the salute was returned. They proceeded to have a conversation out of earshot. Dad and the Sergeant both turned and walked toward me, I was feeling pretty smug. I knew better than to lie to my dad; lies got the leather belt that was in the top drawer. I stood as I had been taught. My dad looked at me and said "I will be back at the end of the day to get you, until that time you'll do what this Sergeant says with out question. Do you understand?" My mouth fell open. I said "yes sir". My dad motioned to the Sergeant who handed me a tire iron and jack from the guard jeep. My dad pivoted got in the car and drove off. I stood there holding a tire wrench and jack. The Sergeant said I would change every flat tire that came to that gate. The Sergeant made sure that I was not reprised or mistreated. I started about 10 o'clock in the morning and kept changing tires until 4:30 in the afternoon. When I ran out of flat tires to change I think he was offering people free tire rotations.

It was the first time I was held responsible for my own actions.

I grew up as a kid constantly moving from one military base to the next, one corner of the country to the next. My dad was on ships at sea 20 of his 27 years in the navy. Having jets flying low overhead is normal. Normal to the point that teachers were use to pausing mid sentence while a jet passed then continuing the sentence uninterrupted. Literally math class was two plus (GR-RRRRRRRRRRRRRRRRRRRRRRRRRRof a jet passing) two is four. The military is its own community, with its rules mores and religions. 50 of the roughly 200 countries of the world have Marine Corps. Half the Marines in the world around 250,000 are United States Marines. In most these countries Marines are commandos or naval infantry. When I was a child there were no police on the base just Marine security guards. On base one set of laws ruled but cross the street and an entirely different set of laws applied.

First and second grade I was living on an NAS Miramar, fighter town USA. Once I woke in Balboa naval hospital I ask

"Where am I?" A man with dark skin and reading a book next to me told me I was in the burn ward at Balboa hospital. He reached over and pressed the call button on my bed. He said the nurse would be in to give me a shot to me back to sleep. The nurse walked in put a syringe in a tube, back to sleep I went. The few times I remember waking up was next to the man reading and a few times for debridement of the burns or testing the nerves. I had stepped on hot coals buried in sand on a beach. At that time state of art medical treatment was to keep me sedated and sleeping so I did not scream. On the same trip, though it could have been another trip, my sister had her face cut open by barb wire on a nearby sand dune. My dad was the CACO, Casualty Affairs Coordination Officer. When dad went to a house during working hours that family left. In the second grade that was my understanding level. My dad went to their house to inform them that the husband was dead. When a plane crashed or was shot down it was two families. Later on I would learn more, a lot more.

Second grade ended with my sister and myself in the backseat of a station wagon in tears. The full emotional fit of losing all of our friends because we are off to the next duty station. Third grade was at a new duty station, not too bad, I remember sprouting seeds in a glass and paper towel. Fourth grade I moved to another school across town, again a new kid new school. I made some friends; I vividly recall playing Brians drum set in one day in class. Fifth grade I went back to the same school where I'd been in third grade. The teacher was my godfather; at least that is what my mom said. He lived next-door to the house I was born in. Math that year was one swat from a whiffle paddle for each wrong answer. I met my first schoolyard bully, Byron. He was a lot bigger than me and liked to run and knock me over with his body. I tried the peaceful approach as we were taught at that age, saying things like "stay away from me" and "don't do that" and talking to the teacher. Pretty much everything failed. I learned to move quickly to get out of his way and how to spot when he was coming for me. Sixth grade was back to my fourth grade school as a new kid yet again. Seeing distant lost friends from two years ago, a lifetime at that age. The bullies were kids from the neighborhood and the school was a safe location I only had to get there and back. My dad was on a ship that year so the parenting was left to my mom. That is where the problems started to show. My mother would hold my shirt or backpack until the bully's had gone past and up the street. I had to go through them to get to school. The times I ran around the house and jumped the fence she would let the bully's know which way I went. Sixth grade I had to learn and adapt. Emotionally shut myself off from failure and punishment. I was constantly set up for it by a parent. Math was divided into one teacher each teaching a separate math classes for grades 4,5,6,7,8. Seventh and eighth grade math classes had a few of the higher testing kids maybe 6 with a low teacher to student ratio. Sixth grade class was stuffed over capacity. Ms Daughterly was the teacher and my home room teacher. My name was at the end of the alphabet. I was in the fifth grade class as overflow with the same bullies I had to fight to and from school. The bullies I made friends with them. I was bored out of my mind and already knew the answers to most of the book. When I could I would get the hall pass under the pretense of going to the bathroom. Sneak past the windows and into the sixth grade class. Borrowing an extra book from the bookshelf, slip in the door, slide in next to the person sitting near the door to learn 6th grade math. That didn't go too well, I was labeled disruptive and a few other things which I don't remember at this age. I was disciplined for not being in the fifth grade math. Mrs. Duncan the teacher decided to paddle me until I cried. It was hard to eak out a tear after spending the previous school year with Mr. Katz and his waffle paddle. Then after five or ten minutes of paddling I got bored and eaked out that tear. A parent teacher conference was called. I was ask what I thought should be done. I stood up for my self and said "I'm really bored in fifth grade math. I understand and know the subject. I did outstanding last year and I should be in the sixth grade math class learning sixth grade math." I was proud of myself. I actually stood up for myself. But the answer from my mother " you never tell an adult what to do. You will be in the fourth grade math class." My mouth fell open. The teachers mouths fell open. I was sent to the fourth grade math class. Fourth grade math class did not consist of math. Instead we traced out lines of our bodies and colored them in. After talking with the fourth grade math teacher extensively and her agreeing that the entire situation was absolutely absurd and damaging I received permission to sit at a desk in the common work room between four classrooms and study sixth grade math through the window of the closed door. I couldn't hear what Mrs. Duncan was saying. I could see what she was writing on the board and missed large gaps in the concept being taught. Trying to get those gaps field at home was not happening. My mother would use schoolwork as a babysitting tool. Home works wrong go do it again. It's an easy babysitter for my Mom. As a child on the receiving end it is a complete mind screw. The concepts that are correctly learned are being unlearned. The parental unit kept saying the correct answers are wrong. It provides hours of fun to an abusive parent.

Later that year I was pulled out of school for a month or two. All the phones were pulled out of the house except one. I spent most days sitting in a chair reading a book next to the only remaining phone in the house. At that time phones were plugged into the wall and cordless phones did not exist. I was assigned the task of ensuring my mother only called my father at work once a day no more. Reason was she would call my dad with a worry such as a plane crashed into his building, my father worked on an airfield that was a possibility, though unlikely. The answer "no that did not happen" Would be met with "but how do I know? or "I don't understand" This would include immediate phone calls back to my dad because it may have happened in the 15 seconds since the last phone call. My dad leaving the phone off the hook switch, which would be met with a busy signal, would receive immediate calls to the next desk, next office, duty desk, officer of the day, commanding officer of the base, or literally calling random people in the base phonebook to chase him down to confirm her unfounded fear was not happening. It became such a problem I was pulled out of school to stop the problem.

Once at a neighborhood squadron get together meet and greet type thing I went to a group of kids my age. I was told "We can't play or talk with you, your mothers that narcissist." I was in grade school I had no clue of narcissist was. That was the first time I was told it was living one. Narcissist thrive on attention. They will continue to interrupt pester harass harm, the list is endless anything to get attention for themself. They will join or enlist other like people to help them perpetuate there insatiable need or want for whatever endorphins it feeds their brain. One of the early coping mechanisms a child learns; is to give the narcissist their 30 seconds of endorphins then mentality shut them off and ignore them.

I was raised in a society with a 50% divorce rate. Any time an aircraft went down 2 to 4 family's would loose their fathers.

Down the street from my house live Steve T. his house had the only skateboard half pike in town. We used to hang out there as kids all the time. His father was MIA. His mother held out hope as long I can remember.

Three years prior to high school graduation my family sat at the breakfast table, on the television were Marines digging through rubble of the destroyed Marine barracks in Beirut. We were discussing who we knew that had just lost their father in that barracks. Four years later I was in meetings with people who were digging through rubble that day recovering wounded and dead. This is the reality I grew up to understand.

BAD BUSINESS PRACTICES AND MANTRAS

This is being added as a separate chapter. It does not fit into the local politics although is practiced by local politics. They are practices and mantras repeatedly observed in practice and are trained throughout business and government. . The effectiveness ranges from effective to annoyances to practices which destroy business.

"Mismanagement is not criminal"
This method of management is usually seen in environments of fealty, abuse and hostility. It is seen and trained in many businesses and governments. It is intentional mismanagement used to drive employees away or measure fealty. It keeps a turn over of low paid employees. Once ingrained into a business or government model it remains. It will be repeated time and time again employee after employee. It builds abuse in the workplace and promotes division among employees. The process uses fealty to find who it will retain and who it will drive off. It rewards abuse and silence. It punishes good business practices. Workplaces which use this bad management practice usually have previously and repeatedly paid fines for the practice. The problem is that the gain is worth the fines to the business.

"Admit Nothing, Deny Everything, Divert, Deflect, Counter Accuse "

This mantra usually shows up interrupting the simplest of business practices. If a restaurant used this practice the patrons would starve. The only way to get business done is to know the counter phrase.

"Patriarchy at its finest. "
This is, depending on the society, an effective means of establishing dominance in business. It usually involves a husband, wife, and children. Tho it can be done with any alpha, beta, gamma group. Alpha begins the business transaction. Beta comes in and interrupts the transaction. Alpha sends beta away. Beta returns, Alpha calls the children to take Beta away and keep Beta from interrupting the business conversation. The Alpha has demonstrated and established their domination. Beta attempts to keep interrupting the business and the children keep pulling Beta away as to not incite the wrath of Alpha and constantly reinforcing the dominance and business acumen. It is very effective in establishing and demonstrating dominance in the business world. It is used daily in many family owned businesses. Failings begin when a Beta without an off switch comes in. Once Alpha has established dominance the Beta keeps coming in and destroying dominance. This occurs when the children or Gamma's depart or are not available. Beta's become destructive when the play is continued throughout the business cycle or continues to the end interfering with the final delivery.

ENGINEER SUPPORT

BATTALIONS

My first duty station was Bulk Fuel Company, 3rd Platoon, 9th Engineer Support Battalion. I was a line walker my job was to patrol pipelines for security and maintenance. Every third month was spent it the field performing operations. The first was a full setup of an amphibious assault fuel system, next was hot refueling helicopters at camp Schwab, another month training army reservist at White beach. The rest of the time was spent cleaning gear, inspections or crawling bars in KinVille just outside the gate. A few times the entire platoon rolled out to KenVille for bar fights. After a year it was back to the states. I was assigned to 7th Engineer Support Battalion. I checked into the bulk fuel company half way through check in I was told to go see the Adjutant. She had a job for me. I became a Legal Clerk which consisted of typing and recording non-judicial punishment. I typed daily "said named member did on or about (date and time) violate articles (list) of the UCMJ to wit;" there was always an article 86, unauthorized absence, thrown in to keep people from taking the charges to court martial. Many of the people I recorded the office hours for were in my old company. After 6 months I was transferred to the armory. The previous custodian was at the end of his contract and exiting service. Day one at the armory the rules were laid out, "what goes on in here stays in here." Most of the people working in the building were corporals one or two sergeants and one staff sergeant. The building was a concrete building with windows a rifle would fit through but not a head or body. The windows had steel shutters which locked for security. Most of the building was filled with racks stuffed full of rifles machine guns and pistols. Marines came to the building once a week to clean them. Once a week or month we would go out to a range to shoot. Most weekends were off. Most days were spent in the concrete building. I did not see daylight for close to 3 months unless through the small windows. One day I said "I'm leaving and going to the beach" to was the middle of the work day. I understood why the guy I replaced took off for two months. Each company had one or two marines as custodian and one armorer per company. It was the late 1980' and most of us were in our 20's. Eventually I had a car first an old beater Dodge Dart and later a 60's station wagon. The car would commonly be packed with people I worked with to go to some club after work. Riverside, San Diego, Temecula, L.A. Tijuana all in a two hour drive. Life was good.

I never considered myself a typical sexual assault victim. I am a 6 foot 200 pound male. When the assault happened I was working the battalion armory as an armory custodian. We worked with the warrior training section a lot. And then average would be on the shooting range about every week or every other week. People I worked with we did some crazy stuff. What went on behind the doors stayed behind the doors. My first attacker was a gunnery sergeant in charge of the S-4.

FIRST ASSAULT

After a drink or two Roland sat down next to me and began talking about his family. I was getting really relaxed. The more I relaxed the increasingly violent the stories became, including holding guns to peoples heads. I just kept getting more relaxed. Soon I was asleep. I felt a tugging on the fly of my pants. I sort of awakened, but barley. My arms and legs wouldn't move as I wanted or at all they just didn't work. The gunny walked to the apartment kitchen and fiddled with a video camera on the counter. I dozed off again then slightly woke to the pulling on my fly again. I could feel his sharp tooth dragging on my skin. I kept passing out and coming to until finally he stopped and wandered off. Eventually I was able to wake up and barely got up I stumbled back to the bathroom. I stood there swaying trying to keep my balance, when he came up behind me. As I finished he took me by the shoulders and pushed across cross the room to the bed. I fell onto it and passed out. I woke up sometime later and got dressed, went out to the other room where Daniel was sleeping on the other end of the large couch. I woke him and said let's go. He drove me back to the barracks. I showered after I got back to my room. I didn't know what to do. I lay on my bed alone in my room until I fell asleep.

THE NEXT DAY

I was awaken by a knock at my door it was Roland the Gunnery sergeant from S-4. He stayed at the door as I did not invite him in. I think I may have said I did not want him in the room. I sat on the edge of my bed with my legs on the floor ready for I do not know what. The pistol I had retrieved the night before was sitting under the pillow. As I write this I do not care to remember the entire conversation, for my health and stability I do not need the memory. He was apologetic and worried. He offered cash for me to keep quiet and I told him I just wanted him gone and the whole subject gone. He left. I stayed in my room I really didn't know what to do. At that time there wasn't don't ask don't tell. If you had homosexual relations you were a homosexual and we're going to be dishonorably kicked out of the service and probably jailed. Homosexual relations were also one of the biggest known kompromats. Entire time he was at the door all I wanted to do was to have this person away from me. I was just trying to stay calm and not be attacked again. From the previous nights conversation I knew better than to let him near me.

BARRACKS PARTY

This chapter is going to be short. The exhaustion of writing this Makes me want to skip this whole chapter. It was thoroughly investigated. People who need to know that information know where to find it. it's not hidden. It was my first PTSD episode. Myself and that First Sergeant were young Corporals having a great night with some great people. Then everything went sideways. All of us were additionally assigned to escort prisoners. Fortunately we had handcuffs about. If you ever wake up after choking on the chunk of meat you just tore out of someone and your handcuffed and hogtied just keep fighting that's what I did.

After I got out of the hospital some of the people I live and worked with got together in a meeting. What precipitated and caused that situation was explained. Apologies were made and accepted. We compare scars, compared what techniques were used on each other and what worked and what didn't. we all left in peace and as friends.

That First Sergeant was not present for this meeting maybe it would've been better if he had been. The relief in that First Sergeants face when he told Jim Mattis how many marines it took to take me out of that fight was apparent. General Mattis looked impressed when he found out. The First Sergeant was glad that fight were love taps to get a private conversation.

While I was in the hospital recovering, part of the recovery process is progressing from having food delivered to your bed to getting up and going eating in the cafeteria. The cafeteria is in the basement of the high-rise building. Myself and the other patients would ride the elevator to the basement. We kept meeting a person from another ward on another floor riding the elevator. This person had noticeable scars on both sides of his forehead. One of us asked if it would be ok if we inquired about the scares. The Marine told us how he received them. One night he was on post and decided to end his life. He drew his 1911 .45 cal pistol, placed it against his temple squeezed the trigger. The bullet traveled in one temple and out the other. We were actually surprised that we were talking to him. He was a person who tried suicide. he said "suicide is not a good option". We talked a few more times on the elevator or at lunch. When I left the hospital he was still recovering and moving forward in life. The conversations we had and what he said about suicide still resonate with me today. "Suicide is not a good option."

SECOND ASSAULT

There's paper on the floor in the top deck common room.

Pretty much from getting out of the hospital I was restricted to the barracks for two weeks and EMI, Extra Military Instruction for two weeks. Restriction was pretty easy stay in the barracks, stay in your room, you can be in the barracks common area, doing laundry, check out when you go to the chow hall and when you get back. No extraneous trips. EMI consisted of picking up trash around the barracks, hallways, stairwells, cleaning the common room and laundry room. As soon as it was done check in with the duty NCO, go back to your room, to read, watch TV, whatever just don't leave the barracks. Occasionally the DNCO would call over the intercom to see if you were in your room. You had to be there and show up when called. Nearest public phone was about two football fields away, in the cluster of phone booths which was the call center, you couldn't go there on restriction so no phone calls out.

PT was over I was wearing T-shirt, silky shorts, running shoes and T-shirt . After PT a health and comfort inspection of my room was done by two Staff NCO' s. They searched for contraband, mattress lifted and inspected. Box springs lifted and inspected, wall locker, every drawer, even the cup holding pens and pencils in my secretary. Apparently writing pens stamped "U S government" are contraband items, at least today they were. What was contraband depend on what day of the week. On Monday a writing pen would be issued, use it Tuesday, Wednesday it was contraband and was admonished for having it. Thursday field day another health and comfort inspection. Friday was either a quiet night at the barracks or a party night Saturday and Sunday everybody slept. Monday PT again.

After the health and comfort I went and checked in with the duty NCO. Did the whole circuit of the barracks with the trash bag, checked the common areas to the top of the barracks and back down to the duty hut. I walked from the top floor downstairs to the duty hut. Upon reporting to the duty NCO I was told there was paper on the floor of the top common room and I was to go clean it up. In the top common room a couple of Bridge company Marines told me to get out of the Bridge company area, as I turned to leave they started to bum rush me. I bolted down the stairs got to the second deck. I got boxed in on the second deck, three coming down the stairs, one or two coming up the stairs, others blocking the balconies on both sides of the building. I ducked into the second floor common room. In one door, I thought I was going to run out the other, when it got blocked. The room is about a 20x40 feet, cinder block walls, roof and floor of reinforced concrete. The carpet a short nap industrial office type in a dark color. The room was painted the latest government issued white or eggshell. Half the room had couches and stuffed chairs the other half a smattering of chairs and tables. There were no sets of anything just individual pieces of furniture. The overstuffed sofas were on the inward most wall. Both doors were on the hallway wall, inset into the room so they opened outward, a window next to each door. One door 8 feet or so from each end of the room.

As I came off the stairs I realized one person was actively blocking me for getting out on the walkway. He came toward me I ducked into the first room hoping he would chase me in the door, instead he went to the second door and blocked the entire doorway. Two of the three people from the room above blocked the other door. They started threatening that I was not going to testify against the gunny. It really quickly went from military to racial reasoning. "You're not going to testify against a brother" That's what one of them said. There was a lot of trash talking going back-and-forth. They were talking tough, I was talking tough back to them. All of us were posturing, shoving, threats and rebuffing threats. One of them said we're gonna bend you over rape you and keep you from testifying. They threatened to beat me, burn me, throw me off the top floor. I kept rebuffing with things I'll kick you ass, fuck off, I'm not afraid of you. The number of people in the room increased and outside other people in the hallway blocking people. Somewhere in all the trash talking, pushing, shoving, I had the bright idea that you can't get raped if you sat down in a chair. I even said it out loud. The biggest of the group we had worked together for the last two or so years. We had been in fights before, usually we're on the same side or breaking up a fight between somebody else. He knew beating on me wasn't going to work. There were other plans at hand. I quickly grab a seat with wooden legs and arms. Wrap my arms around the armrest and wrapped my ankles around the legs. I pretty much locking myself in the seat. They charged and grabbed me. Punches started being thrown. I unwrap my arms and get them up by my head protecting myself from the punches. I keep fighting back which is nearly impossible. Next thing I know my legs are folded into my chest. My legs are being pressed hard into my chest. My diaphragm and abdomen getting crushed. I tried to get out of the chair. I kept fighting. I feel my silkies being grabbed by my spine then pulled up exposing my behind. I grab the front of my silkies and my underwear and held onto them. I realized at that point how bad the situation is and that I could not lose my shorts, literally. Next thing I know my legs are pressed harder into my chest I can't breathe at all. Suddenly I feel something I never felt before. The wind is completely knocked out of me as I gasp. The 6 foot four person I had worked with the last couple of years is thrusting into me hard. I can't breathe my eyes are rolling back in my head my mind is overwhelmed with everything going on. I'm trying to fight, squirm, hit, get away. All my efforts are futile. I can do nothing the stop what's happening. All I can do is hold onto my bunched up shorts and try to fight. Suddenly he stops and somebody else takes his place what just happening begins again. After a few minutes somebody else takes that persons place. By this time I might as well of been asleep on a bumpy plane ride. Except for the occasional knock of turbulence my mind and body completely distanced. I'm vaguely aware when people switched to a point but nothing is registering to me. Finally I hear someone saying "get his shorts off". I'm still hanging on the front of my silkies. It's important that I hang onto my shorts and not lose them. Something else is said. Next thing I know They drag me off the chair and over to the two overstuffed couches by the ankles. They stand on the couches two people holding each leg by the ankles as they stand on the couches. I start coming to and become more aware of my surroundings. I realize that I'm being held in an inverted V. Both hands are holding the front of my shorts, I can't let them go. For some reason them taking off my shorts was important to them. I knew I could not lose my shorts. Finally somebody steps in front of me. Blows are being thrown and I was getting beat. With the urging of the others he rears back start stepping in with a hammer blow aimed right at my crotch. The blow landed right on the cylinder of my .38. I hope he broke his hand. He had no clue what he just hit just that it hurt. That's why it was so important for me to keep my shorts, my 38 pistol in a bellyband holster was in them. Up to this point I'd been unable to get to it. I was folded in half with it trapped in the crease of my body. I started coming around. I was still dazed. I barely knew where I was and slowly gaining awareness to was going on. One hand held my shorts the other barely holding on to the grip of the pistol. After the one guy hit me he was confused as to what he hit. They figured out what it was. They started saying they had to get it away from me. I know I could not let them. They would use it against me and probably kill me. The four people that were holding me started shaking me. The guy that threw the hits was trying to grab the pistol with his good hand. Finally I gained enough awareness to get a full grip on the pistol and take it out of the cloth of the shorts, underwear and bellyband. The shaking became more violent they were screaming. I was screaming, upside down waving a pistol. I was begging pleading screaming for them to stop what they were doing. The entire time I was waving the pistol like a magic wand, it wasn't working. I was still upside down and occasionally getting hit. Leader of the bunch said something to one of the others they left then came back. He went and got an iron. When he put the iron on my foot it was only warm or the burns I have on my feet as a kid saved me from pain. The guy in front of me moved away. I started waving the gun and screaming at the guys who held my left leg. They let go and moved away. The biggest guy, the one who went first, and one other guy still have my right leg. The rest of the crew was to my right some distance away. I remember looking at the biggest guy waving the pistol and screaming at him that I would shoot him. The other guy left moved over with his friends. The biggest guy had my leg in the crook of his arm. His arm like a chicken wing hand on his shoulder. My ankle trapped in the crook of his arm. He started squeezing my ankle. Screaming at me to drop the gun. I was waving the gun screaming at him begging him to stop. Telling him I would not shoot him if he would just let me go. He kept increasing the pressure on my ankle. My leg was burning. I was literally suspended from the crook of his arm. With my free leg I've been kicking him. I finally got my foot under his foreman or elbow. I started pushing with my foot trying to pull my trapped foot and ankle out of his arm. He kept increasing the pressure he was putting on my ankle. He was now squeezing one arm with his other arm. I kept screaming and pushing with my other foot. I took the pistol I've been waving uselessly put it near his body and squeeze the trigger. He screamed, my ears popped. He let go and fell back off the couch he had been standing on. The gun shot bounced off the concrete ceiling, walls, and floor directly into my ears. The scream was replaced by a louder whistling screaming ringing pain. I hit the ground on my back or side or both. He fell back onto the other guy. They both got up holding each other's shoulders. Everyone headed for the door.

I was on the floor alone in the room. I was breathing in sobs my face soaked in tears. I tried to get up the pain in my ankle put me back on the ground screaming. I saw the door I planed on going out when I first ran in the room. I started dragging crawling trying to get up as I headed for the door. I got out the door my shoulder and side hit the rough cinderblock of the hallway. I started heading to the bright light and metal railing at the edge of the barracks. I don't know if I had my shorts pulled up all the way or even if I let go of the trigger of the pistol. I yell down to the duty hut one floor below on the ground floor "duty people are hurt call for help" or something like that. Once twice maybe three times. I grabbed the edge of the rail. I leaned over the rail hooked at my waist looking down at the duty hut. I could see the sidewalk, the base of the window and finally into the window of the duty hut. The duty NCO was sitting at duty desk in the position of attention, logbook in front of him, hands flat on the desk on both sides of the log book, pen on the desk in front of the book, phone on the right corner of the desk. Either side of him two big bridge company guys stood with there arms crossed. I realized there was no help coming.

I begin dragging myself along the rail five or six barracks rooms to my room. My right foot would not straighten out. Every step was more pain. I just kept dragging pulling myself along the railing.

HOLD UP

The barracks room had three beds. Two beds are on one wall. the third bed On the opposite wall, Headboard against the wall to the bathroom and the foot of the bed pointing directly at the door 10 or 12 feet away. I ended up carrying myself, half dragging myself along the railing past the four or six rooms to my room. I was in agony. my right ankle not support any weight It was either dislocated or badly sprained. I don't know about the rest of my body, I was beaten up and bruised all over. I collapsed on the bed. Sometime later There is a knocking on the door. I said if anybody comes through the door I will shoot them. They keep on their side of the door and said "don't shoot it's Williams and Black". They said the command sent them up there to see if I was still alive. We talked for a while and I finally let them come in I think Williams came in and Black stayed outside. Williams got my first aid kit from the top of the wall lockers where we stored our 782 gear. He helped with the cravat around my foot and used the headboard to reset my ankle, a trick my rack mate in boot camp Marin taught me. He helped set my ankle the day before the hump to Bitch Ridge. Williams said the command was going to do nothing about this and they had been told to get their gear and move to a different room. He actually said the command was covering this up. The person I shot was at the battalion aid station one floor below getting care. Williams said official report would say he fell on a price of rebar he was cutting. Right after it happened Williams said battalion pulled a full inventory on the armory. Everything was accounted for. They were trying to figure out where I got the pistol. The crew the command sent to shut me up had been told I was unarmed. I spent a couple of days hold up in the room pretty bad off. My former roommates brought me a couple of meals and some food to eat. They gave me some information. The command was sweeping this under the rug nothing was going to happen to me nothing was going happen to the other person. Unless I gave the command the weapon I was not receiving medical care. Eventually I ended up getting myself cleaned up and dressed in a couple of meals at the chow hall. Someone took a distributor wire from my car. Now I had no way to leave the base. My commute for lack of a better description; wake up in the morning get shaved showered and dressed. My office for the BEQ manager was one floor below me two doors down from where my room was. The stairs at the barracks were choke points. After looking out the window to make sure nobody was outside the door open the door and look left and right down the walkway. It became common to see two or three heads sticking around the corner waiting for me to come out. One day going down the north stairs pocket knives ended up getting drawn. it was a grappling slashing kicking trying to get away from the people blocking stairs. This was right outside the company Gunney's office and the only support I got was a slamming of the window closed so they didn't have to hear what was happening. The gang were actually planning out their tactics to get people coming at me from both sides if I got trapped anywhere I'd have people behind me coming in. I found to get to work; walk out the door of my room, lock it, walk down three or two doors, spider hang off of the balcony, drop to the ground and step to the office as quickly as I could. The office according to the "rules" were off-limits to them as was my barracks room. I had to stay away from the other side of the barracks where they were. Separating us where two cinderblock walls and a 3 foot plumbing chase way.

FIRE ACADEMY

Washington state fire academy Has fire props which require you to travel some distance in smoke and flames to reach the seat of the fire and put it out. One of those is a hallway with fire burning in a room off a long hallway. The hallway has smoke and flames coming down it. The hotter the fire the longer it burns the further the flames and heat reach down the hallway. To get to the fire the crew use short burst of water to push back flame and cool the smoke in the overhead. Too little water the flame shoot over your head and over your crew cooking you with a dry heat. Enough heat is produced to melt face mask, warp helmets and char equipment. Too much water the flames are replaced with steam.The steam penetrates all your protective gear letting heat get to the skin and literally steaming you like a lobster. The important lesson learned is both action and inaction have consequences.

The final exam for the fire academy has multiple test and stages. One is a search of a notionally burning building. On my test the evaluator was Rob Spinner he was going to be my new station captain. Prior to entering the building a selection of tools is laid out to choose from and use during the search of the building. Each tool has its pluses and minuses. A strategy which is taught at the fire academy is to always bring a tool with you. This was a graded test as a student we had to verbalize everything we were doing a quick what we were doing and why. At the beginning of the test I stalled for a long time as to which tool I should take. I went over the pros and the cons of why I should choose one fire tool over the other. I spent an excessive amount of time deciding what tool to take. I quickly learned just grab one and take it with you I does not matter which one just grab one and go. The clock is ticking the longer the delay the more harm caused to people who need help. The right tool is really speed. Just grab one and go.

During my years of fire fighting I repeatedly learned we fight like we train. It played out many times sometimes good other times bad both in drills and real calls. When a firefighter ends up into that type of an emergency situation they respond as they were trained. A common situation is a first engine on a structure fire; officers do a walk around, first firefighter pulls the line to the door, somebody connects in the hydrant, Engineer hooks into the water supply, second team is pulling back up lines, In a short period of time everybody meets at the entrance and entries made. Each member does their part, there's total confidence everything is ready. Firefighters try to keep that to under one minute. The plans the firefighters bread and butter it's rehearsed, practiced, everybody knows what they're doing regardless what position they're in. As a fire captain it frees up time and attention for more pressing matters to be dealt with. Teams are built to that level effectiveness only by working together. There's a term I learned from one of my fire instructors a Hawaiian term called Ohana. Ohana is brothers sisters aunts uncles the whole community working together with one goal and everybody working in that direction. His daughter is the one who taught me how to ride an make rescues on a Jet ski. I became use to working with random people and organizations many times in the middle of the night. Being commissioned as a paid or paid on call fire and medical professional by the State of Washington by the Washington State Patrol has other protections. One hard and fast rules we followed responding to emergencies was everybody that came on that engine or ambulance was going home after the call preferably alive and well.

FIGHT LIKE WE TRAIN

I exited service for two years. I went back in with a reserve air wing unit Marine Wing Support Squadron 472 and 473. They were engineer units for the air wing. Most of my time was spent hot refueling aircraft. The unit also trained to setup Forward Area Refueling Points. Part of the training was to never repeat another Iranian hostage situation. The FARPS permitted us to refuel aircraft at any location in the world quickly.

I cross trained as a combat engineer after the unit was reorganized. The fuel billet went away and combat engineer billets were available.

When NAS Miramar became MCAS Miramar the unit went down to move into portions of the unit to the new base. A group of combat engineers including myself were called to a building. It was in a area of warehouse looking buildings. We walked into a door where someone was holding plans looking at them. We had been called to deal with concrete pedestals in the floor about a foot high by 2 feet by 8 feet. The person holding the plans was confused they said this was listed as an office but did not know where they put desk as the pedestal took up most of the space. I said "Two desk were in that corner pointing to my right. The main terminal was on the nearest pedestal the next room has another row going sideways the drives are in the next room in a U shape." Every one looked at me confused. The person holding the plans "That is what the plans say. How do you know that. I said 'This was the first computer I played on. Its the F-14 Navigation and weapons system. Its my dads old office. I spent a lot of hours in here." shortly after that I changed MOS to computers.

I let the captain Steve know he will be standing in a room with somebody had shot years before. I never gave them the details. Joel showed his true colors. After selling me out, then pulling his shit with "you got raped. you deserve to be destroyed. oh and pack my bags bitch". He found out later why general Mattis packs his own bag.   I am so glad that I found out about Joel before I had to trust him in combat. The response at the COC and later on when one of the Marines out on the pipeline was electrocuted with CPR being performed made it really clear how he move forward in life. He's the type of person that gets ahead by knocking other people down. The moment things are in a clutch he was not going to lead Marines in combat He was going to sell them out. Sell them out not for his life, for his enjoyment.

The first time I was introduced to Joel was at the Marine Wing Support Squadron at NAS Whidbey Island. A tiff started with one of our Master Sergeants, Joel yelled at him " I only talk to combat arms!" The Master Sergeant he was lipping off to had been at Khe Sanh while it was under siege, had a chest full of ribbons and metals including combat action and Purple Heart. That day I found out the S-6 Communications shop at the Portland unit was an incubator for Officers Candidate School students at Portland universities. Joel was holding the rank of Staff Sergeant because he was in OCS, it was a contract rank he was guaranteed that rank for pay purposes while going through OCS. I later transferred to the same unit working in the S-4 logistics office.

Every time I met Joel at professional or social functions It was the same statement "I only talk to combat arms" It was a communications thing that is how he had been trained. When the unit deployed for Iraq I was transferred to S-6 because my military job fell under that office. Joel said the only reason he was on the Marine corps was the uniform it got him laid more at university. His goal was to be a flight nurse. Joel left the Marine Corps to follow his dream of being a flight nurse as a Major in the United States Army. This is what Master Sergeant Michael who training Staff Sergeant Joel later Major Joel had trained him to do. The official policy of the United States Army set by who it hires and retains is "you got raped. you deserve to be destroyed. oh and pack my bags bitch".

DAD'S FRATERNITIES

As a child I went to a Nile circus in Mission Valley, San Diego, California. I was a young child in early grade school introduced to concepts which a young mind could absorb but not understand or comprehend. Parents we're all off someplace else men in one area women another kids in another. One of the chaperones, a person I've never met before, told me to watch the skit that was going on in the main ring, "this is important" he said. The skit was based on the nights of something or another, I can't remember the name after all these years. On a raised stage was a platform with ramps leading up to the ringmaster, Master of ceremonies or maybe even the General of Knights. An amnesty is offered for any nights who failed to show up at the beginning. One hapless knight runs up to accept the amnesty, to rejoin his bride. As the knight ascends to the top of the stairs the ringmaster makes a show of asking his bride if she wants to accept him into the knights. The bride rebuffs, he is subject to humiliation and belittlement. The ringmaster announces that the fraternity of knights are a cocolodry club and fraternity is about being there. The knight is throw down the ramps and excommunicated. I learned things which were completely inappropriate for children. I learned the golden ticket it's really the golden shower. I also learned fraternity is about being there. As I grew up I got to observe and learn about these different fraternities. Twice I remember my dad running into the house saying that an individual missed a first meeting was being offered an in which was a set up for a sex assault charge. Fraternities have some good some bad and all of them have a little bit of both of them. As a fire fighter I learned how the fire fighter fraternity works, EMT's different fraternity with some the same people. Military was another fraternity with different people and rules. Some of the fraternities use the same methods and sometimes for lack of a better term the same clearing houses to enforce rule and punish undesirables. I'm not saying it's right or wrong I'm just saying they use the same process. Some people call it an abuse club. After Vietnam ended some members of my dads cultist fraternity became local politicians some still are today. As I write this book some truly use it as an abuse club. The other members of the fraternity turn a blind eye or activity support the abusers. Fraternity means different things to each individual. Both my parents grew up in the south and as a child and young adult I was never permitted to go to the blue Lodges in the south. Bit too much racism my father said he was definitely right. Sadly that hatred has moved north.

When I returned from Iraq, I took a trip with my dad he took me to one of his lodges, a big stone building; there's a lot of those in and around Washington DC. We wandered through a tower like building looking at artifacts and various displays. One display stood out to me, partially because it filled the center of the room, a mechanical parade. It starts off with the military marching then firefighters police doctors nurses civil servants of all sorts the end of it are the people who sweep the streets. Because it's a mechanical contraption the only way to reset is run it backwards. I was told it takes 15 to 17 years to get from one end to the other. He took me there for a reason I would later come to know.
It was during this trip we stopped at a highway rest stop a mountain pass. The front of the building is stone rip rap which angles up to glass windows about a foot tall to an overhanging concrete roof. The building is cut into the side of the mountain. Inside is it over abundance of toilets urinals and sinks. That day they were cleaning the showers which connect the men's and women's rooms. Those doors are usually kept be locked. Water for the building comes from natural spring on the mountain side above it. No electricity is needed to maintain water pressure. I was intrigued when they explained to me that in order to depart the East Coast on the ground this with one of the few mountain passes people had to come through to go west. The rest stop was built during the Cold War. If Nuclear war ever came or the East Coast was invaded this choke-

point became a strong point and decontamination center. Walk in the women's room from the east, walk out the men's room on the west. Most possessions would be discarded along the way or contaminated to the extreme that only the human being was going to walk through. No possessions, after that point it was who you knew and what you knew. The rest stop was built by one of my dad's fraternities. I literally spent the night sleeping there my way back from veteran X class, The class I've been told about previously. I had a restful night of sleep. The route was suggested by First Sergeant an E-8 I knew. The problem is I do not know which fraternity I should listen to, which is beneficial which is harmful.

FIRST MEETING WITH THE GENERAL

Everything's on the table, wife, career, life. There are control points, rules, laws, plans, procedures and things we do not dream.

The host of this meeting is General Mattis. during previous meetings with general Mattis I was an individual in a large crowd. This meeting was a professional and intimate meeting I went with my wife at that time to a meeting room in a nondescript building in a portion of a town which could be described as all American. I had been to the same place as a child with my parents. The meeting had multiple purposes. One was to introduce and build fraternity with people who were going to work together. The spouses who are going to be remain back could be introduced and exchange information build a fraternity within themselves . They needed a place when battles were going or worse in case somebody was injured or killed. Methods were explained for everyone who went there to have a way back. Everyone who went would come back better then when they departed. After that meeting we had to be at another particular meeting in the future. Being at that meeting was mandatory. If we were not there nobody could talk to us after that time, that holds true even today. That meeting was a check in if we did not check in there was no health care for 10 years minimum, our wives would be required to divorced . It would be denied that we were in the war. A method was explained to make contact and prove who we were if that meeting was missed. It is also explained that are traps. Those traps were specifically designed to put us or whoever tried to replace us in front of a judge have rights stripped and put in prison. The traps included we needed to sleep with a member of the uniform medical corps basically a military doctor or nurse. We were also told this was a setup for a sex assault charge. Easiest way to describe it, we would become an enemy of the state. For spouses there is support training and if necessary what is effectively a witness protection program. My spouse and I both grew up in the military we were already aware of some of this but never to the depth we were going. The requirement was to be published by a certain time to be a 45th. The sex was a distraction I was told.

The meeting was serious though the environment was relaxing. Because we were to be working in the Combat Operations Center. we were given almost indistinguishable tattoos. You could see them if we were in gas mask. It told us who we could talk to or worse who to shoot. It was also our entrance to the golden ticket ball. Any benefits that we couldn't collect because of government service would be distributed at the golden ticket ball. If we lost this tattoo nobody could talk to us. We were taught some kata and physical drills we might need this later if something went wrong. We spoke of classical literature; Caesar, Damien and Pythias and historical military writings. We were given dates in the future to meet up and signals which would be sent. Some of the signals were simple as a phone call others natural phenomenon such as stars and planets lining up others would be manipulations of media such as a news story being printed. A lot of information was disseminated in a short period of time it was a lot to absorb. The plan is everyone in the first battle is going to be present for the last battle of this war. At some point we had a little social time. We got to know each other. Made wagers and cracked jokes. Shane a Marine I'd worked with for years proposed a wager, if somebody could find out about my sex life they would get a promotion. I said no, no bet. General Mattis was intrigued, I could see it on his face, He backed the bet. My sex life and intimate details just became a wager.

SECOND TALK WITH THE GENERAL

You're not a victim if you dominate your attacker.

They just sold me out! I wanted to know if this crew had my back; the answer a big NO! "He raped me, I shot him." It was a simple statement of fact not the entire situation. The entirety is more complex. The last few months my first tour of active duty was spent ditching a gang until my EAs. I had shot one of the gang when they were sent to keep me from testifying at a trial. A Marine Corps barracks with Crips and Bloods having free run. A command letting them have free run. A decade later a crack about my sex life I would take a turn even I did not expect.

I never hid that I went through a rape and everyone above a certain rank in combat engineers knew about me and that First Sergeant, it was just not publicly shared. The communication guys they seem to think rape and brutality is a funny joke, to be mocked the abuse to be continued, this is the leadership from the SNCO'S and Officers. I let the captain know because he really did need to know. I had the OCS class out of Portland thinking it was funny, rape was a joke to them. Comm guy from the other unit kept talking about a First Sergeant the only person in group that a gun shot wound. He kept playing it up. I finally asked him if he was with Bridge Company and he said yes. It hit me like a ton of bricks. They started What What What? I said. " he raped me I shot Him." Rodney ran to the second group after Joel jabbed him and pointed to them. The Lieutenant was laughing and pointed Cabales to the next group. Master Sergeant Michael had a surprise look and had no clue what to do. When Cabales got to the third group I knew what to do. Dominate right now! I started walking quickly where I knew he would be inside. When I hit the threshold of the tent I started calling him out. "Hey old buddy old pal where are you? It's your old buddy Ron!" I was being loud and I was looking for him. Someone said "He's a First Sergeant and you're going show him respect" then started coming toward me. I said "He raped me. You're not him. Get away from me" he tried to grab me, he got flipped. I moved to my left somebody else tried to grab me, they got flipped. That's when I saw him. He had his leg up on the table showing somebody the trajectory of the bullet through his leg. That's the first time I saw the scar. He looked up our eyes met. He recognized me. I recognized him. His eyes went wide then he tried to pull his leg off the table. I went over that table swinging. He started swinging back. Both of use were throwing full force blows. As we were pulled out of the tent still throwing fist I saw Cabales and the rest of the crowd waving their arms and jumping around like school children, clueless frat boys.

After we got pulled out of the tent General Mattis walked over and asked what was going on. He may have actually use an expletive, if so it is the only time I ever heard him use one. I threw my hands in the air palms up. This fight was over I achieve my goal I dominated my rapist. The First Sergeant held his head in shame. He never expected me to come after him. In response to the Generals question I said "He raped me. I shot him." General Mattis ask the First Sergeant if this was true the First Sergeant said "yes". General Mattis said he should court-martial both of us. I said "We've been in the same meetings. We cross the border in 72 hours. We don't have time for a court-martial". General Mattis said "We can do it right here right now." I said "let's do it." General Mattis ask if we are both going to tell the truth we both said "Yes". Myself and the First Sergeant truthed each other out. There was no 5th amendment only Marines following their codes of honor and integrity. The number of people who raped me came into question. I said "7,8,9 I lost count." The First Sergeant said his number a lower number. The general wanted to know the why discrepancy in our numbers. I said "I lost count". The first Sergeant "Said some of the people went twice." I agreed the First Sergeant definitely went twice. So did two or three others. The entire time some guy to my left kept repeating what was said, I said "Its happens. Shut up" a couple of times. He was overwhelmed. The General, First Sargent and myself were having a calm conversation with consequences. The Sergeant Major stood there ready to back the General in half a heartbeat. Somewhere in this I told the First Sergeant I did not know I shot him until today. One of my roommates Williams had told me I had shot him. I apologize to him for shooting him. I told him I was sorry but not completely sorry he deserved it, but I did apologize for shooting him. He accepted my apology I think he apologize too I'm not sure. I actually forgave him right there. I got up in the First Sergeants face I told him "If a squad gang rape occurred again I would execute the entire squad." General Mattis said that will be your EMI. I agreed. I let the General know my frustration, I already lost four Marines due to not being trained to go to combat or because they were female. I had worked with women my entire career they are some of top shooters I have known. I had no problem walking into combat with women. This crew was happy to toss them aside for ego. I told the general about my plan B if everything went south. I said "You and I both know it takes one nuke to knock out all the communications and the entire plan would go south." My back up plan; Me my Marines to go to a marina. Find a sailboat, one with a desalinator and wind generator. I sail back to my wife. All I needed is the occasional quiet beach. I told him the general "When the tides out the table is set." He had a surprise look on his face. He realize that already been through similar survival training the Marines were about to receive. He had a trick up his sleeve, he knew we didn't need the radios for communication, I learned that over time. We started to head back in. I said I was going to take a moment to compose myself. He put two guards with me. I started to walk to cool down and he said watch out for the viper nest. General Mattis put his hand or arm over the first sergeants shoulder and they started heading inside, buddy buddy. One of the vipers struck at my calf. I ripped it off my pant leg and tossed it away. I got bit once I think. The guards followed me. They were bit multiple times. After a few minutes trying to figure out how to get back across that nest, the guards and I decided the closest medical that was safe to get to his back at my unit 500 yards away. As we headed over there I heard general Mattis over the loudspeaker talking to everyone. Part of that included saddling me with the faraday box and ekms. Mattis said if I get that box to camp Viper he would make me a Colonel. I had to get to camp Viper to do my EMI. Until then I was administratively a private. After we dragged each other back to my camp, The guards kept me from getting shot by my camp guards, I still had my mustache. I ended not shaving it off while I was overseas. The protocols I had been having to ignore the last few months we're now in effect. Marines from my platoon came out yelling, it raised me out of the collapse I was going through. I started getting up head throbbing pain increasing. The guards tried to grab me, the Corpsman pushed them down. I got up started screaming at the Marines we're going to have our equipment up and running. I lost the guards then. After screaming at the Marines I went back to my tent, laid on my rack and convulsed. I woke some time later when the rest of the SNCOS returned. I ask for medical care, I did not know where the BAS moved to. Was denied by Joel. He went off on his stuff about males being raped, how they deserve to be destroyed for going through that. He screamed that I was a private and to start packing his bags. He was a contract SNCO going through OCS to be a flight nurse and thought privates were for his personal servitude. It was clear he didn't know very much about military law. Joel seem to think we were rushing for a frat not stepping off to the beginning of the war. I to this day have questions as to the qualifications he had to be a SNCO he leads like he never went to a leadership academy. Over the next two days I watched him getting his stuff together trying to get his section of the platoon up and moving, fortunately he had decent NCOs. Finally the trucks came everyone loaded into them to go to Breach Point West. All the hustle and bustle of the camp was gone. It was quiet.

CONCUSSIONS

Blood vessels are muscles. They are actually muscle tissue. Blood vessels expand contract and are built of the same fiber as the muscles of the body. The brain is full of capillaries, very fine blood vessels. During concussions those muscles in brain tissue bruise. As healing takes place those muscles cramp and spasm just as any other muscle. During my healing some cues or recalls would literally cause a shuttering of muscles cramping where I got hit. It is an odd feeling to suddenly feel shuttering as blood vessels constrict and relax for four or five heartbeats. Sometimes it is as if the brain knows where the information is yet is unable to access the information. Other times it is as if muscle fibers are unaccustomed to functioning in that region of the brain and shutter, like lifting a heavy object to a shelf, As the blood flows in that area while information is recalled. Other times only fragments of the memories comes back.

Head injuries were covered in the first meeting with general Mattis along with some of the failings of western medicine. If we were injured it was known that some portion of eastern medicine would be necessary to truly heal.

Ancient military text from Roman, Greek and before have stories of soldiers with head wounds being permitted to wander off the battlefield. Other stories are of opposing warriors showing up at a missing solders home claiming to have head wounds. Taking the place of the missing soldier and being accepted by a grieving family. Tactics have been devised which sort out which soldiers are real and which are imposters. At a later date the lost and wounded are called back to their general. Flags and banners are hung to remind people where to go. Cryers are sent through the streets to announce the news to remind people where to go. Only the true soldiers know where they must go and what to do. Only the soldiers have been told the path how to get where they must go. The soldiers only need to be reminded. Only they know the time the place the location where they need to be to rejoin their units. Their mates. To be joined with their general once again.

In popular culture the Hippocratic oath says first do no harm. Sometimes to heal harm has to be done. Surgeons cut with knives. Bones broken to be reset correctly. Muscles ripped and torn to stretch them in place. The outcome is the goal not the path to that goal.

Treatments for closed head wounds chronicled in ancient medicine is to keep antagonizing people with head wounds. It is painful and hard both physically and mentally on the patient with the head wound. Detrimental effects can be stroke, inter cranial bleeding, pain, confusion, personality changes and so on. Beneficial effects are exercise, working out and building up blood vessels, the muscles of the brain. Increase blood flow helps flush out bruising opening up and repairing the fine capillaries in the brain. Building repairing muscle takes time and repetition. Eventually route memory begins to return. Areas of the brain cut off by swelling are again accessible in a usable manner. Pain and confusion decrease. Anger and rage responses decrease. What was previously called normalcy begins to return to life.

As an EMT I was trained at a base level about head wounds and their treatment. In the field I dealt with and treated people with head wounds. Sometimes people fell off ladders were unconscious with snoring respirations and all that could be done was to maintain an airway and transport them to a trauma center. Other times it took gentle reassuring and calmly guiding people into the ambulance to calmly go to the hospital. Each call was unique and dictated which care was necessary.

20 minutes after I got hit agitation which raised my blood pressure would change my demeanor from calm level and thoughtful person to a raging, belligerent, highly aggressive person. The more agitation or stress The more inner-cranial pressure, more pain; my response was to become aggressive and belligerent to fight the pain and confusion.

COYOTE TO VIPER VIA BPW

The majority the Marines exited camp. We stayed there for a couple of days getting the remaining people organized, figuring out what best to do. There were a couple of staff NCO's and the Supply Officer. She was a Major who had been sidelined for having a vagina. I figure out what we needed to lift all the equipment we were moving; couple of flat beds, vehicles etc. my guys would runoff come back with what they needed. On one of the sweeps of the camp found a guy sick in a tent. He'd been left behind sick and feverish. I had to go to group to get new cryptographic fills or false ones I'm not sure. I loaded the sick Marine in my Humvee drove by the CASVAC at coyote on my way to group. The CASVAC was easy to find, a freshly bulldozed runway went across the road where the CASVAC was set up. I dragged him out of the Humvee to the triage entrance. I was met by a Corpsman she was chest high to me, the word was already spreading. She said you're that Staff Sergeant who just got busted a private if "you come any further I have to shoot you, I don't want to do that". She said I had to get checked in, motioned over to her shoulder. I told her I have a sick Marine this was a patient hand over. She can said you have to get checked in. I told her to take the Marine. She grabbed his arm. Her eyes went wide, he was burning up. She took him checked to make sure was a Marine, took him to get the care he needed. I left I did not need to be shot and I did not know where to turn in my weapon. I went to group to get the fills I needed. The Crypto tech at group said "I cant talk to you" I said "I know I just need the fills". I went back to my camp after getting the fills. Later the decision was realized that everybody would need to be consolidated at group. My guys packed everything up and got ready to move to Breach Point West.

We received new vehicles which had been stored on the prepositioning ships. One broke down as we started off, the transmission went out. We replaced the vehicle. We were given a vehicle to deliver to the XO at the breach point and an ambulance humvee to deliver to Viper. The road march began in the dark of early morning or late night. The convoy commander stopped at the border. The convoy commander wasn't sure where to go he said 7th engineers should be right here. I told him seventh was already miles ahead of us. They had gone through the breach. The convoy commander split off from the convoy to look for them. We waited at the customs check point, he headed toward Umm Qusr. Thirty minutes later we started to get worried about the two vehicles which had gone forward. In Umm Qusr there were towers which had snipers, cobra gunships had hit the towers earlier, we were still worried about the Marines forward of us. After a while they came back, they couldn't find the battalion they were looking for. We headed to BPW. After we got to BPW we checked in with the company office. I told them I needed ammo for my guys. We had only security ammo not a full load. The Company Gunney L. said there was no M-16 ammunition only SAW ammunition. I took it they don't know why. I inquired about grenades they said they only had incendiary and smoke grenades. I took those too I can burn the hard drives and crypto gear if I needed. Picked up smoke grenades and pop-up flares everything I needed to communicate without a radio. Got back to the Marines and issued out 180 rounds per Marine. I told the Marines to delink and stuff their magazines the last three rounds being tracers and then do four and one the rest of the way. Apparently they've never been taught how to load magazines to know when it's about to go empty and when pull the next magazine for fast reload. The Marines started to realize we were going through the breach into Iraq.

    The 20 foot shipping container of a faraday box got dropped on the ground. The MK142 radio humvee broke down. I was about to get shut down right at the Breach point. I had to push forward. I had the Marines unbolt the radio gear from the 142. The radio gear went into the vehicle to be delivered to the XO. While were doing this the XO came out to claim his vehicle. I was up in his face I said once the 142 gear was in there was a communications vehicle. It was no longer his vehicle. We go to a shouting match. As my blood pressure increased so did my belligerence and aggression. I remember telling the XO there's a war going on and I'm taking this equipment and the Marines forward to the fight. The XO backed down. I got another prime mover to put that Faraday box on. McShea and Vicker were the drivers. After a while the XO came out again he wanted to know why I was not gone already. We headed north with the next convoy. We got to Viper after a long drive. Stoped by the water point to drop off equipment. then rejoin the rest of the unit. It was the middle night when we got there. we stopped our vehicles and slept. Few hours later at daylight we started work. The 142 and mux guys started setting up there communications shot. We found a forklift large enough to pick up the 20 foot faraday box. As we were getting everything unloaded radio chatter about tanks started going on. I had Master Sergeant Michael running back-and-forth across the berm that they built screaming about the tanks were coming. He was inducing panic among the ranks, he had been instructed to do this. We had medium machine guns but no antitank weapons. McShea and Vicker were looking nervous and scared. I told them "ignore him. The tanks are not gonna get here. "Ignore him." Right there that switch in my head put Master Sergeant Michael on ignore. Anything he said from that point on which disregarded as false, It would become a problem later. The driver and A driver looked at me in disbelief. They wanted to know how I knew the tanks wouldn't get here. I told them the fuel farm we're at feeds the ACE, the air combat element. The tanks were in the que to be destroyed. The cobra gun ships are going to destroy those tanks first. They had to otherwise the fuel for the aircraft which we provided, would be gone. The cobra gun ships had to protect their fuel supply to stay alive and in the fight. On my way out I gave the driver and A driver a box of batteries as a going away gift. I began my merry little life at LSA viper. After our communication lines were up and everything running I walked out to talk to the Master Sergent Michael, Joel and one of the gunney's. Got the usual line "we can't talk to you" I told him this was professional, I had my people here how we're going to work them into the watch schedule and I needed medical care. I got more flack back from them. More about me being a private and all the other BS I've been hearing from them. I ask for medical care a few more times got more flack for it. Handed over my pistol twice or four times that got me a beat down but no medical care. Once or twice did the "I just got promoted to colonel your my E-8 here's my pistol get me laid mate." The beat downs ended once I grabbed my pistol or somebody else again. I stopped handing over my pistol and knew help was again not coming. A few times they tried the "you got promoted to Colonel" routine when it came to the "give your pistol to your E-8" my answer was "I don't trust my E-8 I'm not giving it to him." I started doing my work as I could do it. I had stopped trusting the people I worked with.

CPR

It is a look I have seen many times I was seeing it tonight. I lost track of the number of times I walked into a CPR in progress call. There's a look people have when CPR is done for the family rather than the victim. Many times firefighters and EMTs perform CPR to give family time to come to terms, to make the decision it's time to stop life saving measures.

I saw the look on Deb C. face as she was getting the ambulance ready for the next call. It's knowing somebody has to make a decision that nobody wants to make. I looked at her and ask asystole? Deb nodded yes. At the time I was a fire lieutenant or captain, EMT and CPR instructor, the rank was just a tab on my shirt collar nothing more just a rank tab. The car I had just got out of was one of the guys from the South fire district. He was also a fire officer, EMT and CPR structure for their district. He offered me a ride to the hospital from the the scene we had just been at. Once my father was loaded in the ambulance I collapsed both mentally and physically after preforming CPR on him. On the way to the hospital we stoped by a house to drop his kids off. During the quiet of the ride we talked briefly about the realities of CPR. The rest of the time was spent quietly letting the enormity of the situation slowly sink in. An hour before I was having dinner with my dad. The night before I put my ex in jail after she took a swing at me. The swing was the final straw in the march to destruction of our marriage. My dad was at the house when it happened and had been with me the last few days. After dinner, riding the ferry back and walking to the car he started the engine leaned back and went into cardiac arrest. I missed every sign building up to it. I started CPR and other people had been continuing CPR for the last hour. As I walk through the door Rob Spinner one of my fire captains was standing with the ER doctor looking at an x-ray. I recognized the enlarged heart in the x-ray as I'd seen it before 5 Years earlier at my dad's open heart surgery. The surgeon then said his next cardiac may be his last. Rob and the doctor both had that look on their face knowing which decision had to be made. It's the same expression I saw in General Mattis face during our third meeting.

THIRD TALK WITH THE GEN-ERAL

Sons do not live out their fathers sins

The vehicle just let me off. I was breathing deeply trying to get rid of a blinding head splitting migraine and pain I had hard all day. I was trying to get my vision back. The guards had come picked me up I literally could not see to drive. The battle for Nasiriyah had been going hot and heavy. CH 46's had been landing at the casvac all day and now into the night 1 to 3 at a time. They would drop off the wounded and take back off, go refuel or go get more wounded off the battlefield to bring to the casvac. There was a group of Marines near the entrance to the casvac, 15 or 20 feet away from them were two women and a group of other people., To the right General and his group. I already knew I was here for my extra military instruction, EMI and what that was. The general let me know I was there for my EMI. He went on to explain the situation; This squad of Marines brought the injured buddies to the casvac. After dropping off wounded they decided to gang rape, beat and brutalize the female corpsman to my right. General Mattis told me a number which was significant only to a select few people and what the sentence was for these Marines. General Mattis I said I could spend a few minutes to make sure I was ok with this. I went over talk to the girl and the female doctor. The doctor was pretty upset and verbal she let me know what had been done to the young corpsman. The doctor said they broke her face. I talked to the young girl I asked her if what I've been told had happened to her. She looked at me and nodded yes. Her eyes were full of hurt pain, and fear. I checked her face, right side was swollen and zygomatic bone may have moved when touched. She had taken a hard left punch at a minimum. I walked over to the line of Marines and their guards. I asked them if what I was been told was accurate;

that they did in fact raped assault and brutalize the Corpsman? The first three or five marines nodded yes, they had in fact raped and brutalize the young women. I asked them if they understood what type of an offense that was on the battlefield, they nodded yes. Another CH 46 landed and more wounded were carried into the CASVAC. My mind was clear and I knew why the General called me here and what had to be done. My mind is clear like it had on the fire ground. I was about to break one of my golden rules. That rule; never give anybody a reason to harm you. I looked around my mind was thinking like I was on fire ground again. Paying attention to what needed to be paid attention to ignoring what was not pertinent nor a danger. I knew if I did not do this I was dead. A bullet to my head or an overload of potassium in the CASVAC. I still don't know what to do with Nurse Joel. I just knew he had friends in the CASVAC, I didn't. I walked over to the crew chief he was at the end of his tether the other end connected to the helicopter. I asked the chief if he was going for fuel or going out to pick up more wounded. He said they were going out to pick up more immediately. I told him to hold his helicopter one minute. The clock started ticking. I was keeping Marines from getting help they needed. I needed this helicopter right now. I walked back to where the General sat quietly. My mind was racing but clear. I said something like yes I can do this. I said I need to borrow a pistol. I was going to give it to the girl and I may need mine after this. Heads were nodded and someone to the left of the general handed over a pistol. I barely remember checking it. The general said that to carry out the sentence I would need to accept a promotion to field grade officer. You'll be a Colonel after this he said. I replied accepted and said my dad will be proud he was only Lieutenant Commander. I turned and started walking toward the Marines. As I got to the first I lifted the pistol squeeze the trigger. Next step aimed and squeezed the trigger. This went on each step until the number had given me was completed. I hope I stoped at that point. The next Marine I grabbed by collar and screamed "GET UP" I walked him over to the crew chief a few feet away. Told the crew chief over the sound of the helicopter "The next place you pick up your wounded these Marines reinforce that position." I motioned, the guards took the remaining Marines to the rear deck of the helicopter. I think they were four Marines loaded on that helicopter. The pilot in the right front seat was looking my direction. The Marines were loaded. I spun my hand in the air, saluted and pointed out just like on Farps. The helicopter started to lift it off.

My heart was beating like the rotor blades of that 46 just taking off. My vision was going out again. My head was pounding like a taiko drum. I walked to the Doctor and Nurse. I got down by her face. I looked her in the eyes the hurt and pain had been replace by shock. I took her hand shoved the grip of the pistol in it. I told her "This is yours. If you need to use it, use it." She nodded looking at the pistol shocked. I looked at the Doctor also with a shocked look on her face I ask "Can you get her someplace safe? She nodded yes. I said "get her there. GO." They left. I headed for the Humvee. Get him checked in, General Mattis said . I replied "Didn't that First Sergeant teach you anything. USMC, you shoot move and communicate. I just shot I'm going to move I will communicate later". I hopped in the back of the Humvee told the driver move. As the Humvee pulled way I heard the general say get him checked in. I think I passed out in the next few minutes. I woke up back at the fuel farm in front of the COC I got out and walked in.

CHICKENS

Chickens are great come in all sorts of colors and sizes give you eggs, meat and are a joy to watch. Keeping chickens is easy. Give them food water keep their coop relatively clean. Every day Or couple of days collect eggs to eat and cook with. When they are in a clean healthy environment they are relatively self maintaining. Occasionally when you get chicks to raise a rooster is in the clutch. Having a rooster is great with it you can make more chickens it quickly becomes an endless supply of food. Eggs are easy enough to get you just collect them. Meat on the other hand takes a little work. If you eat chicken in any way shape or form you're participating or gaining in the following process, killing chickens. Farm raise chickens do not come in plastic wrap they have to be placed there first. Various books on raising chickens describe a multitude of ways to kill chickens everything from chopping the head off with a cleaver, using cones to chop the head off, Ringing necks, gassing , shooting the list goes on. Eventually when the flock is large enough you're at your point you have to cull chickens. After trying various methods to varying degrees of success one method comes out better than the rest. Chasing chicken is always a fiasco. Ringing necks does not work it is slow painful for the animal and also changes the taste of the meat. It does not kill quickly they only suffer until expiring. Cutting off heads woks on an industrial scale with the right equipment otherwise it is dangerous and gruesome. Quickest cleanest and easiest method I found to cull chickens is to shoot them in the head, preferably with a copper projectile rather than lead. Same method works to protect a flock from coyotes and vermin. The distasteful part is seeing the animal going through death throws. These convulsions happen regardless of the method used. Some convulsions are caused by a lack of oxygen to muscles. Convulsions during death are normal and natural. How human beings respond and interpret convulsions of death are as varied as psychology its self. I have found the best way to deal with the convulsions is to move to the next bird and finish the task of culling as quickly as possible. The entire process of culling I find necessary but distasteful. The general needed to know how I learned to kill as quickly as I did. Why the visual of death did not overwhelm me as it does to so many other people. Food and protection are the only reasons I kill.

COC

When I walked into the COC everyone was jubilant I was just promoted to Colonel. They kept slapping me on my shoulder congratulating me for being promoted to Colonel. My head was spinning, every time I got slapped again the head spin grew worse. The unit which gained the Marines I put on the CH-46 started calling on the radio. The Marines were reporting what had happened to the rest of their squad. The receiving officer was reporting it and requesting medivac for the Marines. I might as well have been in a cloths washer on spin cycle that's what It felt like in my head. The woman they had raped and brutalized was at the CASVAC. I was livid. I told the radio operator to give me the radio. I keyed the mic button. I said "This is stingray actual. Those Marines just got laid. They raped and beat a nurse. If those Marines go back to the CASVAC without holes in them I will personally walk into the CASVAC and put holes in them like I did their friends. Put rifles in their hands and put them back on the line." I dropped the mike everyone was looking at me in shock. Joel had a look on his face his mouth open. Joel just found out how many lives his sell out cost. He also said among other things "they only raped her". I went from livid to off the scale incensed. I started screaming at him. Had those Marines only raped her I might have come to their defense. It was their brutality that sealed their fate. It went beyond pleasure seeking to something else. That is why the General called me out that night. It was something we both knew, I would find out later we both knew brutality and how to stop it. I was up in Joel's face screaming in anger and rage. If I could justify killing him I wound have right there. At some point I told him to get out of my COC and never let me see his face again. I stormed out went to my tent and collapsed.

Later on they drove me over to the kill zone at the CASVAC. Each time they ask me for my weapon, I was keeping it. The entire Colonel E-8 thing was done time and again. The answer was the same "I don't trust my E-8." Once during a sandstorm they brought an ambulance. The engine of the ambulance was revving louder than usual. All I had to do was hand over my weapon step into a brightly lit box at night. I decided to keep my weapon and my life and not be shot that night.

SHARON

On the short drive from the airfield to the CASVAC is the best talk I had a Iraq. It was one of the few conversations I had with anyone. I am glad it was with you. I said something harsh while I was sedated and being questioned, my brain was not healed to the point it is now. I want to sit and talk with you again.

I stood outside the entrance of the CASVAC with you. You were trying to get me to go inside. Flashing through my mind was Mattis saying I was ban from any area which had females because they "don't know what I'd do around women". I remember telling you about being banned from any place with women and ending the statement with "they are idiots". The other is the entrance had become a kill zone to me and it is best to stay out of kill zones. I turned around got back in the Humvee with the two guards then drove back to what I knew. I still don't know if I was the guards prisoner or if they were there to protect me. What I know is they're the only two people I trusted on that barren landscape. There was somebody else in that Humvee that day. You know who she is Sharon. She was the one person I was able to talk to tell what was going on. I think she went and got me help, i just didn't know. She one person who could comprehend what I was going through. I let her carve into me with her razor, one of my most precious thoughts of my entire time there. I think of her and I think of you every time I touch that scar. I yearn deep in my heart to meet both of you again someday.

FORTH TALK WITH THE GENERAL

I had been reading and studying Muqtada Al-Sadr; his back to school program was two to three suicide vest per school. Some real some fake. I had been told it was not "politically feasible" to remove the root of the problem, him. Master Sergeant Michael said "The General wants to see you". My response to Master Sergeant Michael was something like "yeah right sure uhuh" complete utter disbelief. After the tanks thing then being told to go away when I ask for medical care in the first weeks and previous handing my weapon over to "get laid" only to get beat instead of medical care I mentally put him on ignore. No different than blocking a phone number on a modern cell phone or unfriending somebody on social media, he was on my mental block list. Anything he said was disregarded and presumed to be not true. The disregard did not come on suddenly. It progressed through a few learned steps to disregard what he said.

I walked out and sat down. In front of me sat a person who is vaguely familiar. Behind him we're two or four other people. The Master Sergeant who came to get me sat right on my right shoulder, annoyingly close to my right shoulder. I ask " Who are you?" gently he said he was General Mattis. Who he was wasn't registering to me. I asked what he wanted with me? He said I was a Colonel, one of his Colonel's he was worried about me. I needed to get checked in to get medical care. I told him I wasn't going believe anybody that Master Sergeant Michael brought to me. Checking in meant turning over my weapon yet again and that was not happening I was not turning my weapon over to anybody. He balked in disbelief. He said they're serious consequences to the course of action I was about to take. I told him I know but I couldn't believe the person to my right I couldn't explain why. He asked me what I was going to do. I told him I was going to run this just like any other operation; do the mission, retrograde people equipment, demobilize the people. we discussed what my plan of action was he was concerned. General Mattis said he had concerns over letting me return to the United States after seeing me kill people. He said he didn't know what would cause me to kill people. I told the general the only reason I am going to kill anybody is because they stood between me and my next breath. I will breath my next breath they may not. That is the only reason I will kill another human being. There were serious consequences to not getting checked in; divorce, discharge, cut off from peers, no medical benefits for 10 years the list is endless, enemy of the state type stuff. I told him I knew. I also know as told him that if I had had medical care in the first days or weeks things would be different. I had had no medical care in the previous three months not even anti inflammatory. I was having gaps and delays in my ability to comprehend what was going on. Adapting to sudden changes in situations was not happening. There were delays in how I was comprehending situations. I let the General know I had to heal before I came back to the battlefield I made him the offer "Give me the problems that needed removed from the battlefield and anyone who needed to go somewhere else I would put them on a plane and get them out of the war zone. The problems go away and disappear. The solutions go where they needed to go to speed up the campaigns." I think I said I would need a general to back me at some point in the future. Behind him were nodding of agreement or at least that's a good idea.

At some point I ask him why he has flak jacket on backwards, he told me "it was his signature, it would mater later." It was years later when I was reading his book "Call Sign Chaos" that I understood why he wore his flat jacket backwards.
It took me 15 years to realize it was actually General Mattis talking to me that night and additional time to actually write this.

RETROGRADE

Eventually the gear was packed up and the unit headed back to camp coyote. When the convoy left the trip was fun and enjoyment for the rest of the people. Once the platoon was back at Coyote gear breakdown and turn in began. I could not understand why there was no place or procedure to turn in gear.the captain had been talking to me about what types television and popular media I grew up watching. The A-team and Battlestar Galactica and a few others were mentioned. The talks were light not deep subjects. More information exchanges and chat.

One day I had 3 or 4 E-8's sit down and start talking to me. They started making bets with me. I said no bet they said they were not optional they were non-consensual bets. They were putting them as bets to explain what was happening in the future. None of it was to my benefit. It included being forced out of jobs, courts finding against me for any reason, death of family members, destruction or burning of my house. Driving any friends away. The only thing I could do is sell my house and run away. They would force me to live with my mother who is an abusive narcissist. I'd actually kill myself before the last one. The Masonic fraternity of men making better men is formed into an Masonic abuse club. The only way out is to run away and hide or kill myself. They wanted to make sure I was hated and knew it. As time has gone on many of the non consensual bets have come to fruition.

RETURN

Took off from Kuwait international airport a refueling stop in Schiphol Netherlands another in Minneapolis the plane finally landed at March air force base. A bus ride to Camp Pendleton main-side where weapons were turned in. I handed my pistol to a long hair brunette Marine. Spent a week at Camp Pendleton bused to LAX landed in Portland. I thought the battalion commander was doing a great job retrograding. Spent the next months doing martial arts and planning. Soon it was time to transfer back to reserve status.

As I received my New ID card coming off active duty my wife at the time so I need to get Colonel put on my ID Card. She said I was a Colonel.My reaction was "yeah right" "Put staff sergeant on it show me undercover as the person got cockolded out, haha funny." When the clerk handed me my ID card with staff Sergeant on it he said "go to TTF at Bangor".I ask what TTF was and why was I going there? He said he couldn't tell me "just go there".Shortly after that my wife and I got in the car and headed home. Drove up the hill across the overpass and onto interstate 5. As we came down the on ramp we ran into Portland rush-hour traffic. Multiple lanes of stopped cars as far as the eye could see forward and back. My heart jumped I begin vehemently screaming to my wife driving."DON'T STOP! PUSH THROUGH! DON'T STOP PUSH THROUGH! GET ON THE SHOULDER AND PUSH THROUGH!" She looked a me in shock and disbelief. She had just seen how I'd been responding to everything for the last few months since getting hit.

Returning home my wife at the time was angry she said " all you had to do was shave off you mustache and check in." She was right but it never clicked in my brain a lot was not clicking. Returning to Island County went back to my old job as an computer technician. Rejoined the fire department back in my old position. The wife told everyone I was not in Iraq. She even told this to the doctor at the Veterans Administration. The VA did not care about witness tampering or sexual assault trauma at first. After the divorce and my father passing, eventually the VA started giving medications to decrease my anxiety. Nothing was being done about the concussion as it occurred in Kuwait and Iraq it officially did not exist. One of the people in the office at the county also worked at the base. He told people in the office I had not been to Iraq because I did not shave off my mustache as it was a requirement in Iraq. The office staff started pulling stuff to push me out. Thing s like the screen on a computer in Superior court flipping upside down, there is an application for that, walk across the street listen to the clerk say she didn't know how it happened, reset the screen, walk back across the street to my office. To be told it happened again and I'd have to fix it immediately, dozens of times a day.the sane type of thing was going on in the sheriffs office. Management and Human Resources were encouraging the harassment and assault. Any complaints fell on deaf ears. Doctors in the hospital take a different opinion particularly when occurs to EMS personnel which I was commissioned at the time. I hear some people went to jail after I had surgery. After my fathers death my mother started doing the worry phone call routine as she had done to my father. Now she had a cell phone with speed dial. Someone gave her a county internal phone book and a call sheet for the Republican Party which she was a member. The more money she donated the more she could pester people in aiding her abuse of her children. She kept calling the sheriff on his personal line to the point he came to me and said tell your mother to stop calling me. I did, she is a narcissist it only gave her assurance that her abuse was working. Every time she would call him something would go wrong with a computer in the sheriffs office across the street, yet another painful walk across the street.

After being forced out of the county I lived in daily pain worse than in Iraq. My leg had become more painful with each step the mussels stoped healing. Private healthcare was gone and the VA had been working on the problem previously to exhaustion. I applied for social security was repeatedly denied eventually I was assigned the law partner of my ex wife's attorney to represent the social security case this from a county with the management mantra "mismanagement is not criminal. I ended up changing to a closer VA clinic and a councilor from the place where the first meeting with the general was held contacted me. It took a couple of years to work through the built up emotional and psychological problems. I started seeing a Chinese medical specialist and acupuncture. I was getting once a week acupuncture and moxibustion. Moxa made from Mugwart reeks like Marijuana but slowly works, I reeked like a toked up hippy. I decided to join a Marine Corps League for the social outlet. There was a new one forming on the south end of the island. Seemed like a good place to go as it was far from a town where an abusive parent lived. The League president was the father in law of of one of the people I use to work with at the county. I decided that staying away from an an abusive parent was more important than old work animosity's. That changed when his son in law apparently went to jail after I had surgery.

Eventually I needed gall bladder surgery. It took a trip to the local ER in pain to find out. They were going to schedule the surgery at the local hospital. I kept attempting to get the VA to schedule it somewhere other than 2 blocks away from where I use to work. That hospital is a popular place for people at the county to eat. If anyone who works or used to work at he county goes in the hospital gossip about the person spreads like a wind driven wildfire. The last place I wanted to be was incapacitated anywhere near people who had been actively harming me hung out. The last thing I needed was one of the people from the county calling the abusive parent. When my girlfriend had surgery that parent had been told to specifically not visit her at the hospital. The abusive parent started complaining that the nurses would not let her in the hospital room. After failing for months to get the VA to schedule the surgery at an off island hospital I decided to get a restraining order preventing my mother from visiting me at the hospital or while I was incapacitated. I went to the County District Court they did not have forms to fill out. I had to search the internet to find one that worked. When I returned a week or so later I was in absolute pain I was desperate for surgery. I could barley talk was in pain and reeked from moxa. One of the judges came to the counter looked at the paperwork said something like this is that nice old lady at the republican club. Let's go back and talk about this. With my previous dealings with Island county made it clear where this court case was going. It was time to find a different court one that wasn't worried about losing a political donation. That night I had to get surgery, I had been delaying it for over two months. The last two weeks had been excruciating painful. My girlfriends son had been bringing me moxa for the last week. My girlfriend drove me to the hospital. At the only light in town an ambulance followed by a sheriffs car drove through the light. The deputy was eyeballing my car as he turned he picked up the radio. The light changed and my girlfriend drove to the walk in ER entrance. My girl friend pulled into the parking lot. Through the window I saw the clerk get up from the reception desk and headed toward the ER. I got out of the car headed for the door, the girlfriend parked the car. The guard got up flipped the switch on the sliding door as I walked up to the emergency room entrance. He turned walked to a chair 20 feet away and sat down. I started knocking then pounding on the door. The girlfriend had finished parking the car and joined me at the door and started knocking with me. The guard kicked his feet up on a chair. I had enough of island county's abuse the same sheriffs office that had perpetuated witness tampering was not deciding if I received health care. I screamed "NO" reared back gave the sliding door a flat footed kick then another one. The door bowed off the track. I pushed in with my shoulder. Got through the door. The guard got up surprised said "you cant" I yelled at him "GO GET A NURSE." He started walking towards me saying you "can't come in here" hands up like he was going to grab me. I leg swept him to keep away. Screamed at him again "GO GET A NURSE" the third or fourth time a person walked out from the ER. I ask that person "You a nurse?" They replied "I'm an hospital administrator" I said "Get a nurse." Every time the guard came towards me I'd leg sweep and tell him to back off get a nurse. A

Filipina gal walked out said "I'm a nurse what is going on out here?" I gave her a quick rundown of the medical history. She said if I was violent no medical care. Soon I was stripped naked on the floor. The nurse started putting in an IV line. The local constabulary walked in the door and was told to leave they had made enough health care decisions for me. Every time I would get a cramp in my gall bladder I would stop breathing and begin painful convulsions to the point I could not speak. They thought I said gunshot rather than gallstone it got sorted out quickly and soon I was in the ER sedated. Everything from this point on could be a drug induced hallucinations things that's happened afterward made me relive they were not hallucinations. There were a few times the pain woke me up, I would come out of the bed in a fight stance from pain. When I woke from surgery I was feeling the best I ever had in a long time. I was out of pain and feeling relaxed. I ask where I was, someone said the hospital name. I said I have to get out of here I am not safe. Someone said relax think about loosing your virginity. I did, then all the other history hit my brain. I said I have to get out of here before someone comes to harm me. I started to get up. Someone said relax, I stoped took a deep breath then fist flicked the person to my right. I started clearing the room counter-clockwise. Kicked the person at my feet, rolled over to my left cocked my arm back to hit the person near my left shoulder then BAM. The surgery report said I was unconscious and apneic. Apneic is not breathing. The anesthesiologists made me a pile of warm meat on the floor. They put me back on the table and started bagging me with a bag valve mask, the feeling was like going through the second sex assault again. I came back around I would start fighting again. Additional people were brought in to help. They started asking questions and listing the surgical teams in Iraq; it did not calm me down like it was suppose to, this is why getting checked in to Iraq was so important. I said call my doctor. I ended up tied up. The local police found out I had been through sexual assaults started cracking about how much I was going to enjoy prison. The surgical team called the VA. the VA transfer them to my doctor. She said her name, person on the phone said "Oh sorry" and hung up. That person called the VA agin, got transferred the doctor answered, again "Oh sorry" and hung up. The third time the same doctor answer the phone The person on the phone said "hi we're trying to get in touch with this mans doctor. I know you from professional meetings. They keep transferring us to the women's clinic and you." My doctor replied oh "yes he's my patient. He's my only male patient." The surgical doctor said she was confused " your a gynecologist, he is naked on our table and he's a male. Why are you his doctor" My doctor said " he's is a hoot he could kill everyone in the room where they stand. What's going on?" The room fell silent. As a 200 pound male I took that opportunity to start pouring my heart out to my gynecologist. I told her every-thing; What happen what it took to get me to this point, everything including the agreement with Mattis . My doctor ask "you know about what he is talking about" One of the cops Ed a guy I knew from high school, said "yea they kept running him back and forth to his office, said people were taking bets on when I would get force out. He was never in Iraq" I recognized his voice I started going off threatened to come out of retirement and start stacking bodies. That's when my doctor said she had one of the VA police with her in her office as a witness. Things like this happen often enough that it is standard to have a federal police officer present. Ed was now a witness. I was in and out of sedation. The surgical team said something about he's the assassin (that description wor-ries me), we get a woman's clinic. Now a different set of protocols came in. They started fixing things. I could feel when my right calf was stretched. Some other things were done but I'm not sure what. After that I woke in a recovery room. My girlfriend took me home. A couple of days later I went to get roofing supplies I ran into Ed coming out of the local coffee shop he looked surprised, I said hi he said I hope your still in retirement. Thats when I knew the surgery stuff was not a hallucination. Later on at a local coffee stand a woman said to me " I know I'm not supposed to say any-thing about it. Thank you for all you did for the women's clinic."

WHISPERS AND PROPHECIES

Mitchell Oregon 2020, ask for directions to a road with property for sale on it. A young man in his early teens give me directions. The young man spoke with a quiet voice which did not project or carry, to hear the conversation you have to be right there. It reminds me of the voice used when " they " are ever present and listening. The words had so little projection, words said without emotion, no linguistic attention getters, nothing to raise this flow of words and information out of background noise. What do young man said took me about three hours for the whole of the conversation to sink in to realize what was said. I find that so annoying.

There are different ways to teach, learn and communicate. Human beings have a litany of emotions some good some bad. We can control our emotions or our emotions control us. Around 590 A.D. Pope Gregory Put out a list of the seven deadly sins. They are list of the seven heavenly virtues. There are many more sins and virtues than only 14. Pope Gregory also put out the Gregorian calendar supposedly to confuse the uneducated. The whispers I work with and for are masters of emotions. They already knew what emotions are coming in response to a stimulus. Whispers sometimes control which emotions are going to be felt and how people are going to react. Quality whispers are a mixture of psychology, observation, direct and indirect communication. The whispers in the military are the E-8 and E-9's the senior enlisted. In ancient times the senior enlisted would read or recite stories at night to the troops quietly pass information to the troops. Other times sit outside tents of miscreants reciting tales of horror and terror to drive them mad. The senior enlisted have meetings called congresses which is appropriate they are the apes who can beat people into submission. Many of them are trained in psychology. It is a blessing if your on their good list, a curse if on their bad list. Some of the whispers are the same people who cornered me to make nonconsensual bets on my way back home.

GREMLINS

Early December 2019, Heating fuel ran out at the house during a cold snap. My girlfriend and I went to the farm store and purchased 20 gallons of heating fuel enough to last a week until we could get more delivered. We poured the fuel into the heating tank. It was late and cold. The wood stove was keeping the house warm. The decision was made to forgo crawling under the house to bleed the fuel line and reset the furnace until the morning. I crawled into bed with my girlfriend and went to sleep.

I was woken by the back door being jiggled. Next the front door then the kitchen door. Next I hear the crawlspace cover slide back and knock closed against against the outside wall. I then hear the furnace start. Someone had just crawled under the house and reset the furnace. By this time I was fully awake. I stood with my 9mm in hand. The dogs and my girlfriend still slept soundly. I was trying to decide what to do. I was not looking forward to getting dressed going outside crawling on my belly under the house and possibly shooting someone. No step in that process appealed to me. I woke my girlfriend. I told her someone is under the house. I needed someone awake one to call the police if I ran into trouble, as a witness if I had to kill someone that night, she could say what happened. Her reply was "don't worry maybe it is a good gremlin". I was surprised by her answer. I let her know why I was waking her. She replied sleepily "maybe they need a warm place to sleep".

I went out to the kitchen. I stood there 9mm in hand, thinking looking at the floor where the person probably was and looking at the thermometer. It was 14 degrees outside. I was thinking hard what to do. Running the options through my head. Whoever it was they had been there before. They knew all the entrances, where and how to reset the furnace quickly. I finally said out loud "if its a good gremlin, that stays a good gremlin they can sleep in a warm place." I swear that I heard a voice say "Thank you mister." I let the person stay there for 3 or 4 days.

I went under the house a few days later. Something was making noises like a raccoon or something at one of the tighter spaces of the crawl space. I started verbalizing what I was doing and let the gremlin know it was time to move on. I changed the furnace filter and bled the feed line of air. Then left

As time became closer to Christmas my anxiety began increasing to epic levels. Christmas has been a trigger season for me anyway. This year was off the scale, something was driving my anxiety. I went to the hardware store purchased a hasp. I padlocked the crawl space cover, garage and out buildings closed.

My car had been hit in November. The insurance company totaled the car and gave me a check. I used the money on Christmas Eve, bought a one-way plane ticket to my sisters place in Virginia. My girlfriend was upset when she dropped me by the airport I don't blame her she should be upset.

I had to go something was driving me to go I didn't know what. I went to Bellingham airport hopped a flight there. As I was putting the check tag on my bag it tore. I looked around for an airline employee there were none. I walked 30 feet back to the desk. Apparently I violated security they had to make a phone call. I got the tag and flew out. Landed in Seattle to change planes. I checked my bag, a small bag of decadent crystal had broken open in one of the pockets. I panicked, desiccant is round white or clear. This was white to dark sharp crystals which had not been there when I went through security. At Seattle I checked into the gate. I was called up by name. The gate attendant told me I was on the no fly list. They were told to get me on the plane anyway. They had to move me to a different seat.

My seat neighbor was a tall blonde buff marine. He was studying M240 study material. I know the M240 intimately. I have a dive bag for one and "A" bag in my closet. The last thing I told Captain before I left Iraq was " If I'm a Colonel fill the faraday box full of guns, ammo and radios well pass them out at the 20 year reunion. Through that M240 from the humvee on my office wall.". The Plane landed at D.C. national. My sister picked me up at the airport and we drove to Norfolk Virginia.

I ended up in a 12 step program run by the Veterans administration. The program is called Veteran X for males and Veteran Hope for females. A coupe of weeks of class and a medication change I realized I had been told about the class when the congress of E-8's were making bets and prophesies at Camp Coyote. I was told because I was never checked in Iraq if things went wrong we would be sent to a military mirror site to straighten up sober up get clean and get brains working correctly again. The medication change helped decrease the severity length and amount of confusion and shocks.

One of the class participants was a tall dark completed former Marine. He used a walker and had a limp in his right leg. I started to strike up a conversation with him he only said "I cant talk to you." He had lost a lot of muscle weight but it was good seeing him again.

I bought a new car to replace the one got totaled and began a road trip back to the west coast. Spent the first night at the rest stop describe another chapter. Stoped in blue springs outside of Kansas City for a coffee and salad. The coffee shop was full of university students. The young lady at the counter Said to her university age male friend "That guy over there has a scar by his eye. We were told in our sorority if we ever saw a scar like that on someone to call the police they will take care of the problem. But He's not doing anything to call the police I don't know what to do." I had been told the same thing about receiving a specific scar during the a meeting once. After I cleared Kansas City I decided to switch highways just to make me feel more comfortable. I spent a restful night at the Sac and Fox nation. An independent nation with a history of being a stop on the Underground Railroad for escaped slaves, amazing what is learned wandering in a casino. Next stop was a snowy rest stop in Wyoming followed by a night at a quaint motel in Idaho. Left Idaho 6 hours later I was home in a warm house with a beautiful woman. I put the dogs out for the night while I spent quality reacquainting time with my girlfriend. I was awoken from my blissful slumber buy dogs viciously barking followed by voices and thumps. The thump was the crawlspace cover. The Voice said " he put a lock on his crawlspace. Rub some on his door. Let's get out of here. If he finds us he will kill us." Followed by the slamming my breezeway door. They were gone.

The next morning I had an appointment. On the way out I cleaned up whatever got put on the door handle with a paper towel and spray cleaner. As I drove to the appointment I kept getting more confused. The shuttering and disorientation I had lost while I was back East had returned. Someone had been putting drugs in the forced air furnace under the house and on door handles. I don't know how long it had been going on or whom. It did explain why they were concerned about doing something which would make anybody want to kill them. The gremlins we're not good they were bad gremlins.

I still get woken some days early in the morning by someone slamming the screen door. I still do not know who that person is. The amazing thing is that some nights the locked garage door becomes open and the light are on when I wake up in the morning. Maybe it was left unlocked maybe not so a padlock was added to that door. A pair of bolt cutters are kept for when the padlock quits working as has happened two or three times. The nickel and dime harassment gets tiresome, petty people are going to do petty things.

LOCAL POLITICS

Politics are a mix of fealty ego management mismanagement and so much more. It would be so easy to identifiable politics as abusive but it actually does work to maintain power. Local governments work together all the time. One hand helping the other. Courts, police, hospitals, fire districts, phone company's, public works. The full parade of government shakes each other's hands. Bad actors cover each other's backs and help other like actors abuse. People who climb the ladder or are trapped in the fealty trap help abusers abuse. The weak and indifferent keep their heads down and pretend they don't see what is going on that keeps food on their table and a roof over their head. The weak justify it by saying they can't afford to help and the indifferent turn a blind eye to abuse.

Communication among the abusers is diverse, secret handshakes winks and nods do exist. The diverse communication methods protect people by not having someone directly communicated with them. An individual three or four rungs away from any of the parties transfers messages which for lack of a better description have to be "divined". People can honestly say they have had no contact with parties involved in a mater because of the method of communication. plausible denial is maintained. Fraternal organizations are both good and bad. The good is that it protects the people within. The bad is that punishment and harassment of those outside or those to be thrown out is done in a method which protects the fraternal wrongdoing.

Take for example a local fire departments. Most begin as volunteer organizations. Eventually most become full time paid organizations. Many of the paid organizations become unions, specifically a fraternal union. The unions pledge to support each other, right or wrong is not specified, it is a pledge of support. If a person departs one department on bad terms going to another is not going to help the fraternity supports the bad terms. If another fraternity's family member goes to jail for doing something they were not suppose to be doing in the first place the other fraternities help punish the reporting party.

One of the requirement of some fraternities is that a person sleeps with other members. It is a requirement. It gives two options for the fraternity the first is to admit the member the second is to deny the member. There is one group which consist of taxpayer based institutions which uses this method. The "test" is that a person has to sleep with a member's opposite sex partner. In one jurisdiction it is adultery and illegal cross a jurisdiction it is permissible. If the pledge is to be admitted the act is blessed. If the pledge is to be denied the act is rape or adultery a criminal act. I have seen this played out by one of the local medical establishments. A failed pledge goes in for surgery while they are under they are led to believe that a person is going to have their child. They have to sleep with a person to be in the fraternity usually at a casino hotel. The location is important most casinos in the area are located on native reservations. They are sovereign countries acts committed on them are outside the state jurisdiction. Once the person takes the bait a they are drugged and maltreated. In this case the people who do the deeds have state commissions or licenses which if the act was perpetuated in the state would be grounds for jail and license revocation. as the act is committed in a sovereign jurisdiction there is nothing which can be done by the state, courts, and so forth.

CLARIFICATION

Military records show the last highest rank being SSGT.

I do not know who to trust after my experiences. after I received my injury overseas. I ended up isolated in a hostile "lord of the flies" environment which was perpetuated when I returned to CONUS. The fraternity system became a repeating series of hoops to jump through. Sometimes requiring sex with yet another person. It becomes apparent when the path is really a mouse wheel. In one of my fraternity's the sex is a wash out reason in another it is a requirement, I'm not sure which to follow. In the chapter Barracks party myself that first sergeant and the rest of the group had "crossed the line of departure". Another person received a DNA sample from me at viper, that person remains unnamed. What I received from the Portland crew we're sellouts under the auspice of hoodwinking. I came back to people either trying to get me to commit suicide or run off. That was part of the original deal. What was not part was the continuation of tampering and physical abuse. I found out later that medical care was 50 feet away from me. Apparently that medical care was told they were only there to attend to my death and not provide medical care. This persisted even after the Portland crew were apparently ordered to get me medical care prior to check in.

    The courts do not protect tampered witnesses. The courts only perpetuate the abuse of the abusers. The only way I could get the what was occurring at Island County in front of a judge was to file for social security. When informed about witnesses tampering that judge said it wasn't the courts problem. The attorney representing me was partners with my ex's divorce attorney. I later had my ex's divorce Attorney at the first hearing to get a restraining order, he process did not strengthen a lack of trust in the courts it grew that lack of trust in the courts. As a tampered witness every step along the way failed. Those failures stripped the earned and required integrity and confidence of both an honorable General and the courts.

CONCLUSION

After my surgery and trip back to the east coast the head wound began healing quickly. I had removed toxic and harmful people out of my life. Who ever was putting drugs in and on my house is gone locked out or in jail.

My experience with 6th ESB command destroyed the integrity and confidence troops must have for their generals on the battlefield. and later the trust and confidence of judges on the bench.

The leadership of the communications section was culminating an environment that sex assault is fine, perpetrators should be protected and rape victims punished. If any of those people are still employed by the military that has become the policy of the military. Sex assault in the military whether to males or females. Is still handled in a fraternal network which protects the perpetrators. My experience is not uncommon.

I have an advantage I had to pick myself up and get out of torture. Staying in that room where I was brutalized would have meant death. Joel and that command perpetuated the previous commands abused and failures. His elitism would not let him find out he was working with a person who already had two officer commissions.

I was trained to go into deadly environments. If a person was lost trapped or injured WE kept going in until WE brought them or their body out. Either way anyone on the engine company was doing home. That is why I kept going back to the Marines I came in with.

I came home to an environment that was to busy protecting their fraternity to follow anything else. Joel and the rest of the crew perpetuated witness tampering then they had to cover themselves. General Mattis tried to help but got stuck by the rules of the system. At times the right choice is a person to stand on their own no matter what the cost. Twice I had to go to ground to heal. I still have not received care for my back and neck and head.

I forgave in front of General Mattis a person who did horrific thing to me. My current girlfriend could not understand why. That forgiveness was not so much for him but for me, to forgive that trespass against me. The person I forgave is the same person who came when it was time to come out of the depths I had to go through to heal.

The horror that I went through steeled a resolve which cost Marines their lives on the battlefield. A General called me to send the message that sexual assault is an executable offense. That message was carried out to the battlefield.

General your Colonel is ready to return to the battlefield if you need him.

Books for reading

War Secrets In The Ether, Volume 1, Wilhelm F. Flicke
Message To Garcia, Elbert Hubbard
The Trail Of The Fox, David Irving
The Art Of War, Sun Tzu
Enders Game, Olson Scott Card
Constitutional Law, Klotter/Kanovitz
American Practical Navigator, Nathaniel Bowditch

Music for listening

Musicians poets bards and buskers, are as important as authors and many times are both.

Never Surrender, Corey Hart
You Are Alive, Fragma
Life Is Real, Ayo
Let It Rain, Ayo
Fear The Flame, Logan Staats
Rebel song, Tina Dico
Breeze Intro, Xavier Rudd, Live in the Netherlands album
Breeze, Xavier Rudd, Live in the Netherlands album
Spirit Bird, Xavier Rudd
Solace, Xavier Rudd
Absence of Fear, Jewel
Praying, Kesha
Bastards, Kesha
Still in the Fight, Mike Corrado
Wolves Don't Live By The Rules, Elisapie
Bigger on the inside, Amanda Palmer
Footprints In The Sand, Leona Lewis
Bonkers (Feat. Edmee), DHT
Warrior, Hannah Kerr
White Flag, Bishop Briggs

ABOUT THE AUTHOR

Life member of; Disabled American Veterans , Veterans of Foreign Wars, Non Commissioned Officers Association, Marine Corps League. Supporter of Service Woman's Action Netork. Military operational specialties held 1391, 0151, 4066, 0651, 0659 Former fighter fighter, fire Lieutenant, fire Captain, and EMT. Units served with 9th,7th,and 6th Engineer Support Battalions, MWSS 472, 473 and detachments. Worked for Island County, Washington

Made in the USA
Middletown, DE
11 August 2021